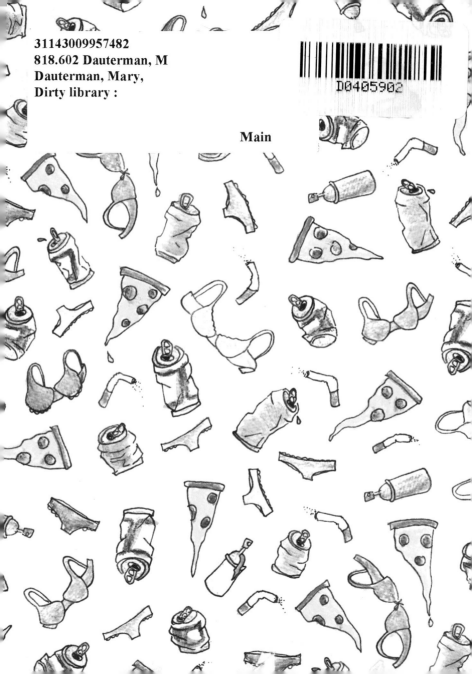

Dirty Library

Twisted Children's Classics and Folked-Up Fairy Tales

Mary Dauterman and Peter Antosh

RUNNING PRESS
PHILADELPHIA · LONDON

Books published by Running Press are available at special discounts for
bulk purchases in the United States by corporations, institutions, and
other organizations. For more information, please contact the Special
Markets Department at the Perseus Books Group, 2300 Chestnut
Street, Suite 200, Philadelphia, PA 19103, or call (800) 810-4145, ext.
5000, or e-mail special.markets@perseusbooks.com.

ISBN 978-0-7624-5440-2
Library of Congress Control Number: 2013958110

E-book ISBN 978-0-7624-5534-8

9   8   7   6   5   4   3   2   1
Digit on the right indicates the number of this printing

Cover and interior design by Jason Kayser
Edited by Jordana Tusman
Typography: Adobe Caslon

Running Press Book Publishers
2300 Chestnut Street
Philadelphia, PA 19103-4371

Visit us on the web!
www.runningpress.com

OMG
YAY!

Contents

Dear Gentle Reader,

It feels like just yesterday that the authors of the very book you're reading were playing tag at recess, and at their desks drawing precious little pictures in crayon. They were such smart, well-behaved little first-graders and I was so proud to be their teacher!

Then I heard that they'd made a wildly popular, critically acclaimed blog (dirtylibrary.tumblr.com), taking classic children's books and turning them into dirty, twisted parodies, complete with new story-lines, original artwork, warped interviews with their fictional authors, and more.

Normally, I would be terribly proud that students of mine had published a book. But I'm afraid that when people start asking, "Where did all the naughty ideas in this book come from?" they'll accuse *me* just because I happened to be their teacher, and just because I happen to be spending a few years in the penitentiary.

I've always held myself to the highest standards as an educator and it would be ridiculous to think that anything I did in the classroom had any influence on this naughty book that they've written.

Surely the adult magazines I kept in my desk had nothing to do with it. (They weren't supposed to see those!)

Or the times I got a teensy bit angry and threw my stapler, or when the police handcuffed me and took me away in the middle of class. Those were isolated incidents and I'm sure that I only had a positive impact on the growth of the children in my classroom.

So in the end, I can only blame their parents.

Sincerely,
Mrs. Finklestein,
Former first-grade teacher
Inmate #18475834

The Bipolar Express

Christmas is right around the bend, and the stress of toy-making has put Kris Kringle on the crazy train. . . .

Excerpt:

*'Twas the night before Christmas and all 'round the pole
Not a worker was sleeping, not one goddamn soul.*

*All the elves in the workshop were in quite a pickle,
All due to that "Saint," that boss who's so fickle.*

*And where was that chief, once nice, now a dick,
Where could he be, that unstable St. Nick?*

*He was not in his workshop, not down in his lair,
But instead at the shrink, in the psychiatrist's chair!*

*To tell you the truth, Santa felt pretty low,
He wanted to resign as Pole CEO.*

*He'd yelled at the Missus and lashed out at the elves,
He screamed, he shouted, he hurled toys from the shelves.*

*He cursed so loud that the words from his mouth
Carried as far as that Pole in the South.*

*His voice shook every stocking, every last jingle bell,
"I fucking hate Christmas! All you kids go to hell!"*

*And now lay Santa, on the couch of some quack,
Needling and wheedling for some Prozac. . . .*

Dear Santa,
i am SORRY you are feeling bad.
How is rudof →

WHEN i get angry Mommy
says take a chill pill. Maybe
ast a doctor for some chill pills.
i want a ~~Bob~~ BARBY House and
a Millyon dollers $ $ $ $
and some $ $ $ $ $ $ $ $
chill pills. $ $ $ $ $ $ $
Bye. $ $ $ $
Missy (i am 6)

13

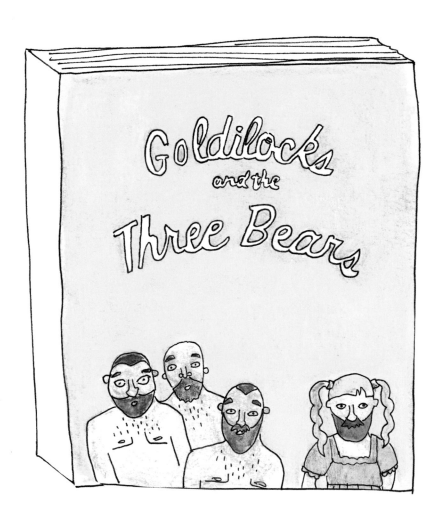

Goldilocks and the Three Bears

Goldilocks is wandering through the woods and happens upon a house owned by three large, manly bears. She walks inside and samples their food, sits on their furniture, and tries on some of their more intimate garments. When the house-mates return home, she tries to run, but she's soon captured and, as it turns out, Goldilocks is not what she seems to be. . . .

Reviews:

"A queer tale and, I might add, a bad one."
  —*St. Louis Post-Dispatch*

"Bad news bears! Thumbs down, way down."
  —**Harold Bloom, Yale University**

"Surprisingly intimate."
  —**Stefan, Grindr Beta User**

Where's Dildo?

Sandra has had a long, hard day at work. Now that she's home, she just wants to get off with some solo mojo. But her room is an absolute pigsty and she can't find her vibrator anywhere! Can you help Sandra to climax by finding Dildo?

If you enjoyed *Where's Dildo?* you might also like:

Sex Toy Word Search
69 pages of hide-and-sexy with words and sexpressions about your favorite instruments of pleasure!

Connect the Dildots!
Follow the numbers with your pencil and watch the phalluses grow right along with yours!

The Lyin' Bitch AND THE Wardrobe

The Lyin' Bitch and the Wardrobe

Told through the lens of a mall security camera, this book captures the tale of little Lucy Pevensie, a compulsive luxury-store shoplifter. Lucy, so cute and seemingly innocent, can talk her way out of anything—but can she outwit Aslan, the new mall-security dog?

Word on the Street:

"I didn't like the book very much so I stole it."
—**Winona Ryder, unemployed actress**

"You'll find the book security tag between pages 120 and 121."
—**Convicted shoplifter, name withheld**

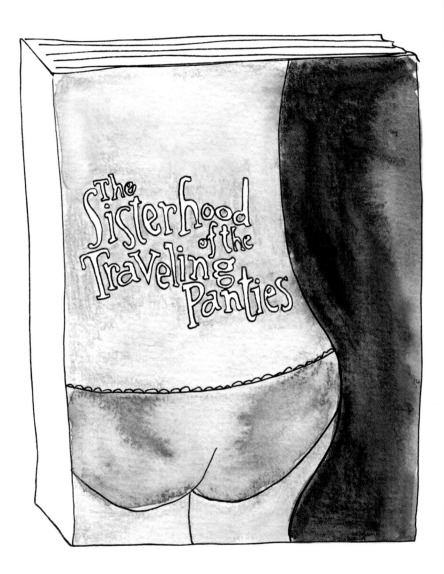

The Sisterhood of the Traveling Panties

When four high dollar, globetrotting escorts meet at a Las Vegas bankers' convention, they realize just how much they all have in common—hair (blond), dresses (skimpy), STDs (all of 'em). Then and there, in the City of Sin, they form the Sisterhood.

Reviews:

"When it comes to love, it don't matter if you bought it, it just matters if you got it."
—**Charlie Sheen, psychiatric test subject**

"A strong candidate this year for the highly coveted Hooker Prize in Literature."
—*ClitLit Monthly*

The Magic School Slut

A new bewitching girl is raising all the boys' magic wands at the uptight Wizard Academy. Her magic power? Making virginities disappear.

Book Club Discussion Questions:

- What spell did the girl use to drop all the boys' pants during the pep rally?

- Do you have your own "magic" move that you like to use in the bedroom?

- Does this book jacket make me look slutty?

Three Billy Goats' Snuff

Billy Bob, Billy Joe, and Billy Ray are just three kids who like to dip chaw all day. But the evil troll guarding the checkout counter tells them the legal dipping age is eighteen. Now the Billies will have to use all their country wiles to outwit the checkout troll and get their dip on.

"FREE COPY with purchase of five or more tins of
Cameltoe® Premium Fine Cut Tobacco."
—Joe's MegaSmoke Shop

Green Eggs and Hammered

An odd-looking man with a funny hat is afraid to try new foods . . . until his friend Samuel gets him very, very, very drunk.

Excerpt:

Will you eat them with a beer?
Chase them with some Everclear?

Will you take them with some wine?
When you're drunk they taste divine!

Maybe douse them with hard liquor?
They will go down so much quicker!

Would you? Could you? In a bar?
Chug it! Chug it! Here they are!

Word on the Street:

"Getting wasted really did help me to try new foods. But it didn't help me to keep them down."
—**Theo, 24, picky eater**

"Getting your children drunk is a great way to get them to eat their spinach."
—**Brandy R., teenage mother**

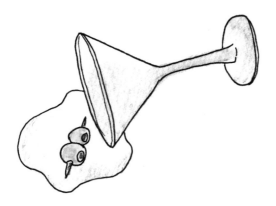

Puss in Booze

Puss the tomcat's swashbuckling adventures are long behind him: His fur is mangy, his belly sags, and his arthritis keeps him from getting into his world-famous boots. Now he's spending what's left of his nine lives sitting at the bar getting drunk as fuck. But if you can catch him when he's slightly sober, he can still recapture a little of that old magic and tell you one hell of a story—for the price of a double bourbon.

WARNING:

DO NOT ACTUALLY GIVE
YOUR CATS ALCOHOL.

BECAUSE THEY WILL LOVE IT.

Review:

"FAS (Feline Alcohol Syndrome) is a serious problem in the feral cat community. I was so outraged that this book was making light of it that I coughed up two hairballs."
—**Susan D., president of CLAWS**
(Cats Lovers Against Wasted Strays)

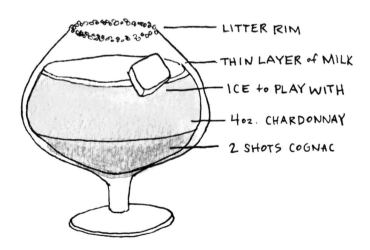

LITTER RIM

THIN LAYER of MILK

ICE to PLAY WITH

4 oz. CHARDONNAY

2 SHOTS COGNAC

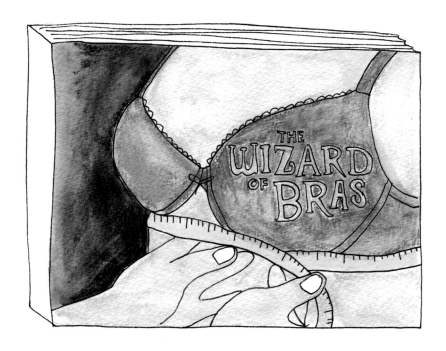

The Wizard of Bras

Busty young Dorothy is feeling low because she just can't find the right brassiere. So she heads down the Yellow Bra Road to the mall to see the "wizard." This flamboyant store owner may hide behind a curtain, but he can guess any woman's cup size and always finds a girl the support she needs.

Reviews:

"An uplifting tale, sure to push up any girl's self-esteem."
—*CosmoGirl*

"Those ruby red slippers just didn't go with any of her undergarments."
—**Tim Gunn,** *Project Runway*

PUSH-UP
great for
MORAL SUPPORT

BALCONETTE
great for
EMOTIONAL
SUPPORT

BRASSIERE
great for
CHILD SUPPORT

Mary Pill Poppins

Mary, a mysterious governess with a haughty attitude and a bottomless bag of prescription drugs, blows in with the west wind, and answers a family's call for a new nanny. Her unconventional child-care techniques—along with a spoonful of Valium—win them all over and have a profound calming effect on the rambunctious kids.

Excerpt:

"A spoonful of medicine helps the children go down," whispered Mary Pill Poppins as the two little ones swallowed the syrup and drifted off to dreamland.

Review:

"Although at first controversial, the pharmaceutical-based approach to child care has proven very effective."
—*Babysitter's Quarterly*

Little Bo Creep

Little Bo loses her job as shepherdess after misplacing an entire flock of sheep. Her newfound free time only feeds her addiction for stalking, but nothing seems awry until severed sheep's heads start appearing around the village, and the nightmare has only just begun.

Book Club Discussion Questions:

- Was the farmer's death at the hands, er, hooves of a flock of sheep all that it seemed? Or was Bo Creep involved?

- Have there been times when you've been driven to random, vicious murder? How did it feel?

Reviews:

"Like Michael Myers's mask in *Halloween* and the shower in *Psycho,* Little Bo Creep's small, gore-soaked shepherd's crook is destined to become a symbol of horror."
—*St. Louis Post-Dispatch*

"... a total rip-off of every book I've ever written."
—**Stephen King**

The Little Engine That Came

None of the big and powerful electric train engines will help a poor farmer move his heavy load, so it's up to one little steam locomotive to help out. But with his tiny whistle and a slight case of ED (engine dysfunction), no one believes in him but himself.

Testimonial:

"The inspirational tale of how positive thinking can overcome even the hardest (or least hard) problems. . . ."
—**Lee Bido, MD**

If you enjoyed *The Little Engine That Came*, you might also like:

OverCome
The story of a famously flaccid mountaineer
who, facing seemingly insurmountable hurdles, rose
up and mounted them. First Everest, and then
his new bride.

The Flimsiest Excuse
How one husband lied to his wife about his
impotence while carrying on multiple affairs behind
her back.

Beauty and the
Cease and Desist

A beauty pageant winner discovers that she has a
secret admirer . . . and takes legal action.

Book Club Discussion Questions:

- Why wasn't Beauty DTF? Was the Beast totally groady?

- Has the law ever gotten between you and love? Based on your own experience, what advice would you give to the Beast?

- Did you find the story about the Beast's curse plausible? What curses have you been under?

Reviews:

"Attacks modern privacy issues head-on."
  —*ACLU Book Review*

"After the book's release, our privacy blinds and window-tinting sales skyrocketed."
  —**Al's Window Wonderland**

Alice in Wonderbra

Precocious young Alice falls into an enchanted underworld full of talking animals, wacky teatimes, and magic potions that supersize her bust. She'd be happy just to get home in one piece, though a new bra wouldn't hurt. . . .

Other titles from the same author:

Through the Looking Ass
Journey into the magical world of proctology, the hottest, dirtiest field in medicine!

Up the Rabbit's Hole
Get to know one of nature's friskiest animals, and follow the adventures of the White Rabbit as he tries to get some (cotton)tail!

The Jabberstreetwalky
The famously hilarious poem about the whimsical lives of urban good-time girls!

the Pied Piper

The Pied Piper

An unemployed, disgruntled rat-catcher takes revenge on a rat-free town by handing out tobacco and pipes to children and teaching the kiddos how to light up, taking them down the long road of addiction, never to return.

Testimonials:

"An addictive tale that will have you going back to it again and again."
—**Philip Morris Inc., spokesperson**

About the Author:

Mr. Nicholas O. Tyne has written more than a dozen children's books about tobacco in the past twenty years. He is the target of several ongoing lawsuits involving his controversial Smoke for Schools Foundation, which advocates cigarette breaks in elementary schools to combat childhood obesity.

The Jungle Bookie

Little man-cub Mowgli is having a hard time adjusting to life in the jungle, until he makes some new friends and teaches them about the joys of gambling. The orphan becomes the bookie for the jungle and quickly works his way up to a jungle casino.

Testimonials:

"A great way to introduce your children to basic concepts like winning, losing, and winning big!"
—*Gambling for Dummies and Small Children*

"Chock-full of numbers games to teach the kids!"
—**PokeHer67, online poker player, substitute teacher**

If you enjoyed *The Jungle Bookie*, you might also like:

The Adventures of Double and His Dog Nothing
Follow mischievous young Don Double and his faithful puppy-sidekick, Nothing, as they get themselves into trouble and have to risk everything to save their young hides!

Encyclopedia Brown and the Case of the Thrown Game
He may not be old enough to grow a beard, but this boy-genius knows point shaving when he sees it.

The Hunger Gamers
Their parents won't give them allowances, but that doesn't stop the Hunger Gamers club from betting their lunch money on crap games. The stakes have never been hungrier!

Huckleberry Gin

Tom Sawyer told him he needed to go to rehab. Becky Thatcher said the hooch was ruining his complexion. And Aunt Polly and the widow Douglas banned him from their homes. Well, Huck told them all where they could go, because he was headed down the Mississippi—just him, a song or two, and a whole bunch of booze.

Word on the Street:

"It's not the slavery, intolerance, or racial slurs that bother me—I just can't tolerate drinking."
—Helen, 94, Women's Christian Temperance Book Club

"Like, I just really liked the like symboletry of everything the book means and like America and like independence."
—Veronica, high school junior, who didn't read the book

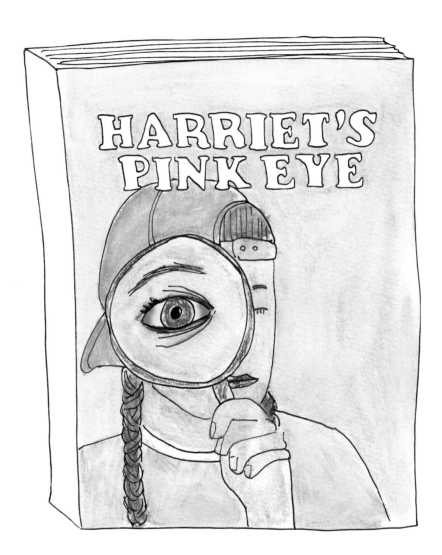

Harriet's Pink Eye

Fourth-grader Harriet has always wanted to be a private eye, but her snooping is just fun and games until she uncovers a career-making clue. There's a big-pharma conspiracy to infect all of New York City with *Bacterium Conjunctivitis*—more commonly known as "pink eye." It's up to puffy-eyed Harriet to unmask this evil plot and save the Big Apple from a hideously crusty fate.

Review:

"... yet to achieve widespread popularity, but now, in its third edition, it has proved a sleeper hit with optometry schools."
—*Publishers Weekly*

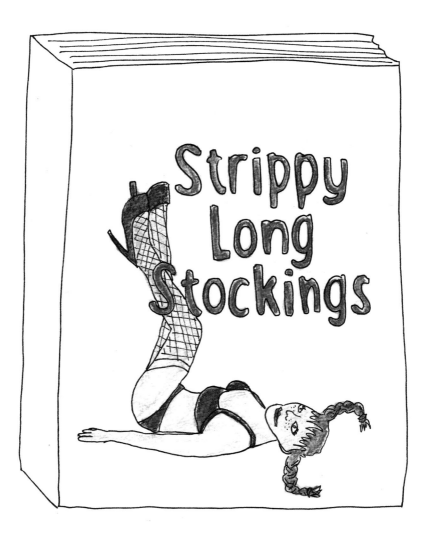

Strippy Long Stockings

Men from all around the world come to the red-light district to see this redhead dance. But don't let the girlie pigtails fool you, fellas: Miss Strippy is *all* woman. And the only thing this lady loves more than putting on her famous gartered silk stockings is taking them off.

Testimonial:

"A landmark book for redheads! We are rapidly making up ground on blondes and brunettes in the imaginary girlfriend department."
—The Red-Headed League for the Promotion of Gingers

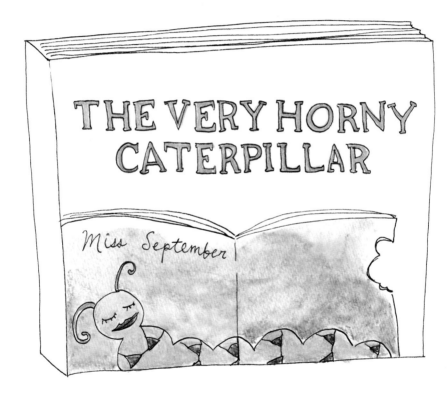

The Very Horny Caterpillar

Fresh out of the egg and ready to get humpin' on life's adventures, this is one frisky little caterpillar. He's humping everything in sight, but when he tries to hump a hungry sparrow, the very horny caterpillar learns that, yes, you can have too much mojo.

Review:

"Caterpillars are the larval form of the butterfly and are thus not sexually mature and cannot be sexually aroused: *D–*"
—**Children's Science Book Ratings Authority**

The
Goose Who Laid
the Golden Keg

The Goose Who Laid the Golden Keg

A fraternity buys a goose to be its house mascot, and the frat brothers are delighted to discover that it produces the most wonderful beer, one red Solo cup after another. The fraternity brothers assume the bird must be *filled* with beer, and, in an effort to get drunk faster, they unwisely cut open the bird, mortally wounding the goose who laid the golden keg.

About the Author:

A. Soph is the pen name of a brother in the Tappa Kegga house. He is also the author of *Keg Stand: My Upside-Down Drunk College Life*, which can be found in the philosophy section of your local bookstore. He enjoys beer pong, tailgating, and debates over which is better: Keystone or Milwaukee's Best.

Johnny Appleweed

The classic tale of that all-American pothead Johnny Appleweed, who walked barefoot across the American West sowing his dank marijuana seeds and pioneering pot legalization wherever he went.

Testimonial:

"Johnny was truly one of America's forgotten founding fathers—the cornerstoner on which this great country was founded."
—**Abraham Lincoln,
private correspondence, 1863**

If you enjoyed *Johnny Appleweed,* you might also like:

Mary Jane Eyre
A narcotic biography about Mary Jane Eyre, from stoner adolescent to small-time dealer.

Blunt Force
It's dealers versus cops, vying for control of the streets in this thrilling board game of chance, skill, and dope!* This hand-painted and carefully crafted game board features 420 spectacular colors that will mesmerize you as the game blazes forward and the stakes get higher!

*Ages 18 and up (Mary Jane not included)

MAKE an APPLE BONG!

① YOU'LL NEED:

 AN APPLE

 FOIL
(POKE HOLES
IN THE MIDDLE)

A PEN
SHAFT
(EMPTY)

③  INSERT THE
PEN SHAFT
(MAKE SURE
TO REACH
THE CORE).

④ COVER CORE
WITH FOIL.
PLACE
WEED IN
BOWL.

②  CORE
THE
APPLE.

⑤  ENJOY.

Handjob and Gretel

HJ and Gretel get lost on the back roads after a little "road hand." They can't find anywhere to stay except the mysterious Gingerbread-and-Breakfast.

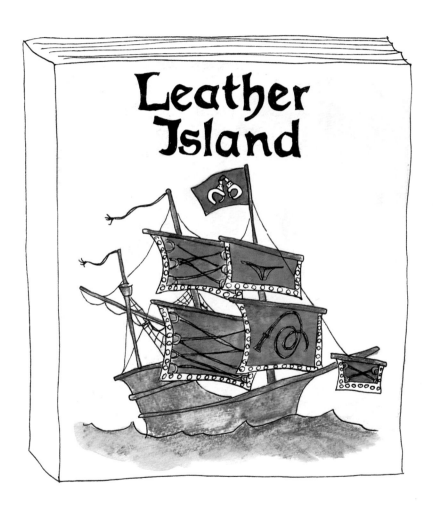

Leather Island

Young Jim Cockins finds an old treasure map in his mother's brothel, and sets off in search of booty with a hired crew on board the *HS&M Domination*. But once out on the ocean, the ship is hijacked by the ruthless Long Schlong Silver and his pirate seamen. They place Jim and the crew in fuzzy handcuffs and set the ship on a course bound for the infamous Leather Island.

Knot-Tying Guide:

Before handcuffs were invented, you had to be pretty good with the ropes if you wanted to have a little submission-and-domination fun. So here's our tip sheet for getting *knotty* with some old-school S&M.

The granny knot: For those who like their ladies well beyond cougar, we recommend this classic bond.

The double fisherman's knot: First developed by amorous anglers, this tie-up is perfect for those sexy times when you're looking to get entangled with two others! A great beginner's orgy knot.

The constrictor knot: If you're into erotic asphyxiation, then you'll be out of breath for this twine tie!

The coital coil: For when you want a little *kink* in your rope.

GRANNY KNOT

CONSTRICTOR KNOT

DOUBLE FISHERMAN'S KNOT

COITAL COIL

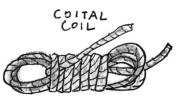

Jack Off
the Beanstalk

Jack, a dim-witted farm boy, trades the family cow to a traveling salesman from the city for a handful of magic pills that promise to make his stalk grow. Foolish Jack takes them all at once and when he starts beatin' the ol' beanstalk, things—well, one thing in particular—start to get out of hand.

Review:

"... a terrifyingly accurate depiction of a Viagra overdose and the horror of the six-hour erection."
—*AARP* newsletter

Old Mother Huffer

Everyone's favorite grandma is back and badder than ever! She's cashed her Social Security checks and she's off to the hardware store to get herself some "party supplies"!

Excerpt:

Old Mother Huffer
Was starting to suffer
'Cause she hadn't had her paint,

But she huffed some glue
(More than she's used to)
And started to feel quite faint.

Testimonial:

"I didn't read it, but I can tell you that the glue in the book binding will get you high as shit."
—Jeff, HuffPo correspondent

Clifford the Big Rabid Dog

Big ol' Cliff is at it again and he's got the whole town in a tizzy! An encounter with a sick raccoon leaves Clifford feeling a little weird, and when he wakes up the next day he's downright crazy! Follow the giant pawprints and the pools of dog slobber and watch as Clifford plays chase with the people of the town, turning them into human dog chow!

WANTED
Eager young postman.
Athletic types preferred.
No references needed!
Avail. to start yesterday.

Clifford

THE BIG RABID DOG

Who needs a vet? Check for these signs to see if your dog might have rabies:

- Inability to bark

- Lack of appetite, only has thirst for blood

- Disinclined to engage owner in intellectual conversation

- Depression

- Confusion

- Prefers scratching you, rather than being scratched

- Excessive salivation, to the point of being inappropriate

- Insomnia

- Spends all day and night playing dead

One Fish, Two Fish, Dead Fish, Blue Fish

That much-loved, freewheeling tale about death and dying is back in this new twenty-fifth anniversary edition!

If you enjoyed *One Fish, Two Fish, Dead Fish, Blue Fish*, you might also like:

Necro Phil
Till death do they part. And maybe not even then. . . . Phil's love for his wife goes beyond the call of duty . . . and beyond the grave.

Chicken Soup for the Soulless
From heartless strangers to passionate stranglers, these new tales are sure to chill even the warmest, most bubbly person!

Dead Man's Float
Harold, the grown-up son of the local undertaker, runs the most popular ice cream parlor in the county. His splendid sundaes have everyone dying to know how he makes them. But it turns out that the only ones who know his recipe . . . are in it. . . .

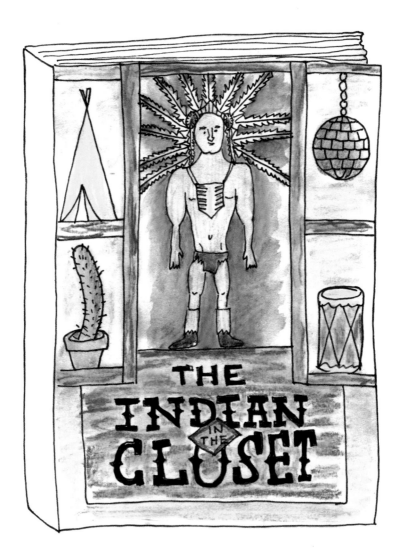

THE INDIAN IN THE CLOSET

The Indian in the Closet

A curious little boy is disappointed when all
he inherits from his grandpa is an old wardrobe.
But he soon finds that it holds a secret power—it
makes whatever you take out of it just a little
more *faaab–u–lusss!*

Reviews:

"A new take on the well-known coming-of-age,
time-travel, magic-figurine story."
—*Publishers Weekly*

"A gorgeous allegory of how the Indian from the
Village People got his start, we think . . ."
—*Los Angeles Times*

Five Little Junkies
Jumping on the Bed

Five Little Junkies Jumping on the Bed

This wild quintet used to jump to get high, but pretty soon that wasn't enough. They go from being adrenaline junkies to actual junkies, caught in the up-and-down life of addiction.

Excerpt:

Five little junkies jumping on the bed,
One OD'ed, fell down, and bled,
Mama called the doctor
And the doctor said,
"No more heroin or they'll all be dead!"

Testimonial:

"A much more long-winded PSA than the classic, Drugs Kill."
—**Meth Max, local pusher**

Where the Girls Gone Wild Things Are

Set sail to an island full of your most feral fantasies, where getting wild has never been more fun, exotic, or topless. Call now! Only $19.95! Must be eighteen or older to order.

From the Official Website:

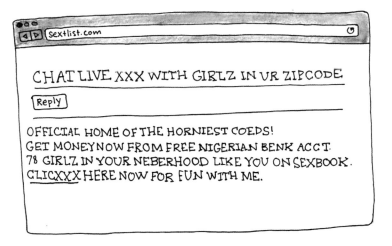

Word on the Street:

"Loved the book's positive, playful portrayal of condom use."
  —**Planned Parenthood**

The Pervy Little Puppy

John and Lisa think it's cute that little Fido has learned how to use their desktop computer, but one day when they find something sticky on the keyboard, they realize that their adolescent dog has been enjoying a different kind of dog treat on the Web.

Most popular Google searches among pups:

- Milkboners
- Doggy style
- Best of Rear Sniffing video
- Wet poodle webcams

Reviews:

"Contains important lessons for children, like how to clear their browsing history and cache."
—NPR's *All Things Considered*

"Pornography offers young dogs an exciting alternative to the typical chair/leg humping."
—*Dog Fancy*

Are You My Baby Daddy?

A lively educational romp that teaches the importance of paternity tests for parents of all ages through the story of the desperate Mama Bird looking for that rascally absent Papa Bird. Recommended for ages puberty through menopause.

Review:

"A Grade-A Whoddunit."
— *Chicago Tribune*

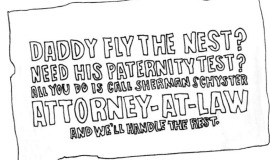

DADDY FLY THE NEST?
NEED HIS PATERNITY TEST?
ALL YOU DO IS CALL SHERMAN SCHYSTER
ATTORNEY-AT-LAW
AND WE'LL HANDLE THE REST.

The Ugly Duckface

A teenage girl's desire to fit in goes well beyond overusing the latest lip gloss from Kmart.
To truly fit in, she must not just *do* the duckface, she must *be* the duckface.

About the Author:

Born and raised in Beverly Hills, Mrs. Barbara Kenn is a recovering plastic surgery addict, a struggle she chronicles in her stunning autobiography *Thinking Outside the Botox*. She now operates the charitable foundation Knives Take Lives, which warns schoolchildren about the dangers of excessive plastic surgery.

Little Boy Blue Balls

A young shepherd boy's dreams are perpetually haunted by a voluptuous city woman. It wouldn't be so bad if, just once, Little Boy Blue could manage to blow his horn.

Excerpt:

Little Boy Blue,
Come blow your horn,

There's girls in the meadow,
And girls in porn.

There's girls on the TV,
And girls on the Web,

We're terribly sorry
They're not in your bed.

Review:

"Tantalizing, but ultimately unsatisfying. . . ."
—*Boston Globe*

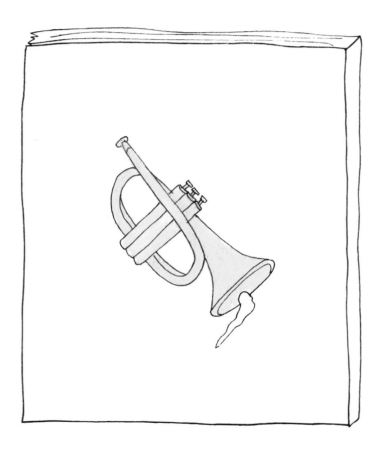

If You Give
a Mouse a Roofie

If a hungry little traveler shows up at your bar,
he might order a margarita. If he orders a margarita,
that creepy stranger in the corner might send
him a drink. . . .

Reviews:

"If you are looking for action-packed, this is not
the book for you. Not much happens after page 2.
Love scenes are tastefully executed."
—*Philadelphia Inquirer*

"I put down the book not feeling very satisfied, but
not really remembering why."
—*New York Review of Books*

About the Author:

Mr. Sneaky Pete McGillicutty is the author of six books and the center of controversy concerning the film adaptation of his latest novel, *Morning After*. Movie studio executives claim they have "no recollection of ever signing a film contract with Mr. McGillicutty."

Alexander and the Total Fucking Bullshit Hungover Day

Alexander's wild night with Everclear, Four Loko, and other suspect liquors is sure to give you flashbacks to the migraines, puking, and regret of your first hangover, and have you hugging your toilet all over again!

Review:

"Word to the wise: Don't get the pop-up edition."
—**Oprah's Book Club**

Often purchased with:

Advil; Gatorade; *Have We Met Before? My Blacked-Out Life*

Alexander's Bar Tab:

```
  BARFLY'S
  BARF + GRILLE
  - - - -
          2:30 AM
  - - - -
  BEER          7.00
  BEER          7.00
  SHOT          9.00
  SHOT          9.00
  DOUBLE SHOT  20.00
  DOUBLE SHOT  20.00
  SHOT          7.00
  CHARDONNAY   12.00
  SHOT          9.00
  BEER          6.00
  SHOT          7.00
  PIÑA COLADA  16.00
  CHARDONNAY   12.00
  SHOT          9.00
  BEER          7.00
  DOUBLE SHOT  21.00
  BEER          7.00
  BEER          9.00
  PIÑA COLADA  16.00
  MARGARITA    16.00
  SHOT          9.00
  BEER          7.00
  SHOT          9.00
  SHOT          9.00
  - - - -
  TOTAL: REGRET
```

Little Whorehouse on the Prairie

The Ingalls girls are lonely pioneer daughters, desperate to find love and earn a little money the old-fashioned way. So when a new frontier army outpost brings unexpected business to the Ingalls household, the good times roll and bring acres of laughs!

Reviews:

"And you thought modern bras were hard to get off."
—*Washington Post*

"Pioneer life sure sounded hard."
 —**Ms. Ratherbottom, first-grade teacher**

"Oh, how I long for a Prairie Home Companion."
 —**Walter, Pioneertown reenactor**

"It's fun to imagine Michael Landon doing the love scenes."
 —**Jeanette, Frontier Book Club president**

What's Your Slutty Pioneer Name?

First Name:	Last Name:
A- Adelia	A- Ass-Lass
B- Bunny	B- Bosomgown
C- Constance	C- Curly Girly
D- Desdemoana	D- Dirtytalk
E- Ezekiel	E- The Endowed One
F- Fanny	F- Feelsgood
G- Gertie	G- Got er Done
H- Henrietta	H- Heavens Me
I- Ichabod	I- The Innocent
J- Josie	J- Jackov
K- Kandace "Kandy"	K- Klapp
L- Louisa Maye	L- Longfellows
M- Mercy Me	M- McFeelsy
N- Nimrod	N- Nakedbottom
O- Odessa	O- Oh My
P- Prudence	P- Pantyless
Q- Quincy	Q- Quickie
R- Rosabelle	R- Rippedbodice
S- Sus-Ahh-nah	S- Sweetspot
T- Tabitha	T- The Hot One
U- Uriah	U- Underdrawers
V- Viola	V- Vagninah
W- Willamina	W- The Whip
X- Xeraphina	X- Triple X
Y- Yankel	Y- Yee Haw
Z- Zola	Z- Zipadeedodah

Good Lord, Moon!

The midnight sky was covered in clouds, but
one special little boy will still look out the window
and see a full moon. (And he'll spend the rest
of the night buried under his covers, completely
terrified.)

Excerpt:

Goodnight, brother

Goodnight, mother

Goodnight, bunny

Goodnight, money

Goodnight, spoon

And good night, moo—AHH! WHAT IN THE HELL IS THAT AT THE WINDOW!?

Testimonials:

"A classic bedtime story to keep any munchkin in bed and away from the windows."
—**Chelsea, the worst babysitter ever**

"No need for monsters under the bed when you have a book this terrifying to kids. . . ."
—**Maria, mother of six**

The Giving and Receiving Tree

Since they were little, the boy and the girl have always met and played at the big apple tree on the corner. But as they grow and mature, the old tree becomes a place for a different kind of play. (And the tree gets in on the action, too.)

Readers' Poll: The Top Five Sexiest Trees

5. The Date Palm
Popular among arborists for one-night stands

4. The Banana Tree
Enough said

3. The Fir
The female fir tree sports some pretty ridiculous cones

2. The California Redwood
No wood has a bigger trunk

1. The Coconut Palm
Who doesn't want to handle those giant coconuts full of milk?

Bi-Curious George

George has always been a curious little monkey. But lately the cute chimp has been raising more than a few eyebrows (and other body parts) since he began experimenting with a whole different type of banana.

Curious Ape Facts:

- Humans and bonobo chimpanzees are the only land mammals that make love face-to-face.

- Both male and female chimpanzees typically mate promiscuously and all year long.

- Forty-seven percent of all chimpanzees admit to having paid for sex in the last five years.

Sweet Valley Gets High

After 152 books' worth of adventures,
identical twins Jess and Liz tire of all the teen-y
drama and just want to mellow the fuck out.
They move into their parents' basement, bringing
with them a newfound passion for snacks 'n'
blunts, and adding a new chapter to their
never-ending chronic(le).

Review:

"Full of offensive stereotypes about cannabis users.
Puff, puff, pass on this book."
—*High Times* **magazine**

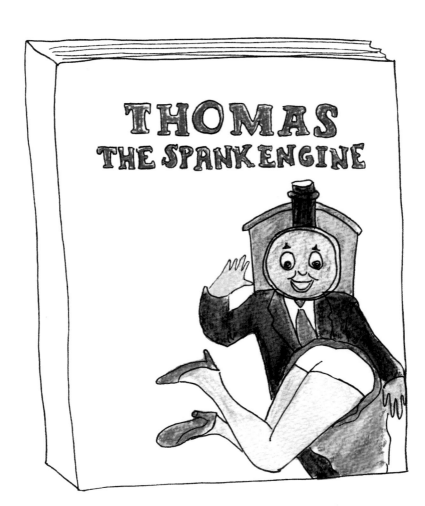

Thomas the Spank Engine

Thomas pulls mile-long trains across the country all day—mind-numbing work that has him ready to go off the rails. So when Daddy gets home, he's got a one-track mind and he's ready to let off some steam.

Reviews:

"Sick, twisted, and morally bankrupt. In short, I loved it."
—Bill O'Reilly, *Fox News*

"I read it to my child, but strangely she hasn't been speaking the last two or three months since. I wonder if I did something wrong."
—Tina J., mommy blogger

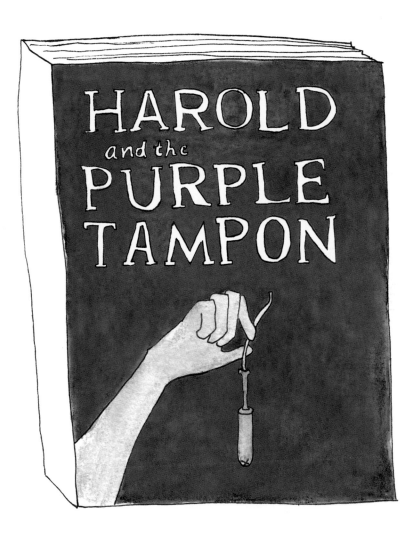

Harold and the Purple Tampon

Curious little Harold spends the day playing with his newfound pearlescent plastic purple toy—which he calls "Tammy." But poor little Harold's world is turned upside down when he's told what "Tammy" is really for, where babies come from, and the biology of the human reproductive system.

Testimonials:

"Women do that?? Once a month!? I had no idea."
—Jordan R., adult male, single and looking

"BLOOOOOOOOODDDDD"
—Local metal band, lyrics inspired by the book

Acknowledgments

To Allison and Adriann . . . is this real?

To Jordana, our amazing editor; Jason, our designer; and the team at Running Press for printing this on actual paper.

To our parents, who believed in us a little too much.

To email spam filters: Give us our emails back.